Darktown Follies

Poems

Tupelo Press
North Adams, Massachusetts

Darktown Follies
Copyright 2013 Amaud Jamaul Johnson.

Library of Congress Cataloging-in-Publication Data
Johnson, Amaud Jamaul, 1972–
[Poems. Selections]
Darktown Follies : poems / Amaud Jamaul Johnson. -- First edition.
    pages cm
Includes bibliographical references.
ISBN 978-1-936797-39-4 (pbk. original : alk. paper)
1. African American theater--Poetry. 2. African Americans--Poetry. I. Title.
PS3610.O316A6 2013
811'.6--dc23   2013025770

First edition: November 2013.

Cover and text designed by Bill Kuch of WK Graphic Design.
Cover art: Portrait of an African American comedian, circa 1900. Lithograph. Created by
The Courier Lithography Company, Buffalo, New York. Used courtesy of the Library of
Congress Prints and Photographs Division (http://www.loc.gov/pictures/collection/var/item/
var1994001731/PP/).

Tupelo Press
P.O. Box 1767
243 Union Street, Eclipse Mill, Loft 305
North Adams, Massachusetts 01247
Telephone: (413) 664–9611
editor@tupelopress.org / www.tupelopress.org

Tupelo Press is an award-winning independent literary press that publishes fine fiction, nonfic-
tion, and poetry in books that are a joy to hold as well as read. Tupelo Press is a registered 501(c)3
nonprofit organization, and we rely on public support to carry out our mission of publishing
extraordinary work that may be outside the realm of large commercial publishers. Financial dona-
tions are welcome and are tax deductible.

ART WORKS.
arts.gov

Supported in part by an award from
the National Endowment for the Arts

for Hayden & August

C O N T E N T S

The Walk Around

The Olio

THE WALK AROUND

"*Somebody hasta black hisself*
for somebody else to stay white."

—Melvin B. Tolson,
from "Sootie Joe"

Encore

Take the architecture of the wrist,
how the hands flit, hinged

& bony as a blur of wing pulling
each egret across the slow drag

of the lake, or the way the whole flock,
given the hound dog's solfeggio

& the report-refrain of some pistol,
how each tendon, how every muscle

of the limb seems to reach
some agreement & move.

Even the box seats & the balcony,
the taste of that song tangled

like moss about my Adam's apple,
& I see them beginning to stand

& applaud, & if I could spoon
out every eye, or fasten their tongues

like red scarves around a flagpole. *Think,*
come morning, the both of us, rich men.

So I wait for them to release
their bellies, to rest their elbows,

to stop slapping their knees. I adjust

my top hat, smooth my hands

against my breast & tail. I step
center-stage. I *steady,* I *steady*

& bow.

The Front Matter

Pity the ringdove, the silver-tongued
Coxcomb, throb and pulse, the hurly
Burly of the hurdy-gurdy man. Pity
The pomp, all the prunes and prisms,
That miscellany of light located beneath
The lips and gums. It's all that cockeyed
Peacockery, the dumb show high flown,
Guffaw, and that garbled moonlight.
Now, I got the big talk. I'll play the heavy.
Watch me in my cap and bells, my jingle.
In a nutshell, all patter and ballyhoo aside,
I'm aping the Sun. I am the Jack-pudding.
I reckon to *out herod Herod,* and trademark
My move.

He Swallowed an Egg

Mr. Cleveland: seems like I got this shell
      Nestled up just above my abdomen.

Damnedest thing, the shopkeeper's touch.
      What you think bring a man

Into the inspiration to get all catlike,
      Like that? Was whole under the custody

Of my tongue, then before I know, gone.

Say, the moon's nothing but blown glass,
      And god just gone and hid the straw.

Say, the heavens just like my hands
      After I've bled the hog good and clean,

And stars, like barley fanned out across the coop.
      Here's my predicament, cousin: if I move,

The egg will get the lion's teeth,
      If still, then come all the waiting

Until that Shanghai rooster begins to claw
      At my belly, until he starts to itch for air.

Nobody

"The man with the real sense of humor is the man who can put himself
in the spectator's place and laugh at his own misfortune."

—Bert Williams (1876–1922)

Bet you showed 'em, Bert.
I mean, got their goat good
the way you pulled that fist
of fifties from your billfold
& bought the whole bar
a round. Trace of burnt cork
coloring the edge of your collar
& your smile, sliced wide
as a melon's quarter moon.
I see their faces, outcropped
& looming in the darkness;
cigar smoke cross-hatching the air,
& shadows clustered, all leaning
in corners like small congregations
of drunks. Light from the Lafayette's
marquee, *Abyssinia,* & the red lettering
of your name wasn't enough to stop
the barkeep's ribbing. "Mr. Nobody"
you sang, "O Death, Where is Thy Sting"
& you, cakewalking with your eyes,
pantomiming something like laughter.

Two Real Coons

Act One:

Daresay there was little difference
Than playing the Moor, a second skin

You thought, an accent. Your wife sitting
At the stage door dressed in ermine,

Her hair in some fashionable torrent
& your face, three ovals, glazed, spinning.

But it helps to think of the little tramp,
Purblind and choking on coal dust,

Knapsack dangling like a wasp's nest
At the end of a stick. Next stop, Cairo.

Smell of Black-eyed Susan. Train tracks
Stretched-out like some iron vertebrae.

Next stop, Cedar Rapids, Chattanooga.
All teeth & bloody gums. Lookout Mountain,

Look out into the crowd, the night, & your
Walleyed audience, & try to keep your nerve.

LeRoi Eating Watermelon at Howard

Better dead. Better to dig up and foul
Poor Booker's bones, or pluck the pearled
Buttons from the good Doctor's waistcoat
Than undo all that fine book-learning.
What rancor, boy. What black and wooden
Alchemy would bring you into the clear
Light, seed-spitting, meat, juice smattered
About your mouth and neck? Better to petition
Fools. Better doxologize a devil even, than
Abandon the good sense God gave a chimp.
This here is the whole caboodle, "Capstone
Of Negro Education," and you, collar undone,
Hair in pothooks, teeth damn near gnashing
The rind. Son, I aim to write down your name.

Miss Thelma

Our butterfly, our fancy warbler,
Roiling in a scramble of night.
O sweet oblivion, honed.

The body's bounty & the heart,
Trilling. All that soft weight burning,
A pulse of light, the smell of camphor,

Splayed. The song centered around
How the fire flapped its tongue.
O cobalt heart. Satin baby doll

Inked out & twirling on a twisted
Spoon. Her voice like a sparrow
In a pillbox. Hear, how the shadow

Palmed the sun, how it scoured
Wood. She slept nude. O
Bone-rattle. Augusta, our Thelma,

Our song, unfolding.

Fancywork

Picture her, the Black Patti—
A black soprano, a wunderkind,
Lovers like medallions, bossy.
In burgundy, studded maybe,
After the dog acts and acrobats,
Maybe in white gloves, she
Walks out, begins *Faust* or *Martha*.
Did they notice her back, the arrow
Of her voice, those hands, ringing?
Mama's little songbird until
Miss Lady began to lionize
Those notes, their brocade, her lungs,
Her breath, ornate and lingering
long after the wash. Then the Grand,
The Orpheum, men chewing their
Fat cigars. Someone will say *the air
Was baroque.* Their eyes, a gaudy
Mosaic, and her voice, a hurtle.
Even Garvey, general of no nation,
Starts tittering where he sits.
Nigger Heaven, and the applause
Like some broken idiom.

Pigmeat

Come to this common fallow of bone,
This body, hulking—this billowing robe.

Midday & the moonlight across my face.
Come: these hands, this beat, the broad

Hiccup, a smile. Here, when all the heat
Has been washed & wrung clean from the body

When the men begin to open their leather cases
& hold their monocles a little closer to my heart

& the parable of the homegrown &
The parable of the artificial Negro

Will be told. Here, with the sweet broadax
Of history, the thunderous applause.

Here comes the first crystal stair.
Here, come Hell or high-water; Hell

Or some falter. All the ease in legalese.
Here comes my tautology—

A blackness of a blackness of a blackness.
My monochromatic rainbow,

Articulate as a single finger haloing the moon.
A generation, spun-out or spooling & I'm dancing.

Here. Step. Stutter-step, hush. I come.
Here comes the judge. Here comes the judge.

It's the Kingfish, Honey–Pining

So I'm telling this fella at the package store
About Sapphire, and how sometimes I get
All muddleheaded with want. See, like, how
Back in Marietta I was the cat's pajamas,
A high muckety-muck. *My Cherry*. (Now,
I'm talking to Sapphire in my finest, genuine
Castilian French), *My Cherry*. And she's cutting
Her eyes. Her dress, cornflower, I think.
And I got my best hat in my hand, friend.
The music. The floorboards on her Mama's
Front porch, keeping rhythm like, *Sweet* and
Sweet and *Jesus*. And I say, "you ain't never
Need to want for house money, again." I say,
"We can fashion us a mighty fine honey-pot,
North." Hear me out, Andy: it's not when or how
The woman slaps you, that sting, like an eyetooth
First breaking the skin, it's waking up twenty years
Later, and finding your nose is still wide open.

A Blues for Miss Lucy Jane Stubbles

"I've been abused, I'm all confused . . ."

—Ernest Hogan, 1896

And I need you home, back in Shake Rag.

All night, the hour—the wind, clicking
    Its split tongue against the front window.

And that second hand, needling my heart. *What's he got?*
    When spring last came to Kentucky,

You were opening boxes stuffed with whalebone and pearl.
    And I wrote you songs. I put folding money

In your purse. And now, it's the trail of your powder, escaping
    Like air through a pinhole in the lung.

Tomorrow, I'm gonna tear down this wallpaper.
    Buy me one of them one-way tickets out

To Richmond. I'm gonna sell my daddy's mouth
    harp. I'm gonna get me a line on a gun.

Clarence Muse Stars as The Magical Negro
in Francis Ford Coppola's *The Black Stallion* (1979)

Since the story begins with sugar,
the dark and muscular storm
of a horse, and its epicurean propensity
for sweets, who could be surprised
when you emerged from the mist—
your hair, the cotton-white smoke
of hellfire, that toothless, tangerine
gummed *click, click* to move your buggy
along this Lexington back alley,
this dirt road River Styx.

I think we were meant to love you;
just as the boy, who should not have
lived, keeps roping his noodle arms
at the base of the neck of The Black.
Yes, there's prayer and ship fire,
the long sequence of trust in the burning
sands, that gallop like a locomotive
strumming a harp. The Black. The Black.
And my oldest son, for once, silent
in our basement's sixty-watt gloom.

Bootlick (or a Love Song in Defense of Lincoln Perry a.k.a. Stepin Fetchit a.k.a. Gummy in *Hearts in Dixie*) (Fox 1929)

I know what you got knotted
up in that cakehole. I can tell
from the fretwork of those bloodshot
eyes, and all that iron you got laced
in your gait. You come to wrench
a reckoning; you come, maybe, to unhitch
my soul from its blue-suede and patent-leather
mercy seat. Come on, don't get all mealy-mouthed
now on me, son. On set, when Selznick asks
for a grin, what I give, I got Jupiter gnashed
between my teeth. Selznick says, *cower*
and I call this arm, here, my bow-string,
and I bend, and I make this body,
frame and membrane, this whirling
dervish of dung and bone, I make myself
a makeshift mandolin, I imagine a pauper's
harpsichord, and I let them play.

Then Butterbeans Begins "The Itch"

To watch Butter settle
into his trademark spin
and scrawl, to watch
the hard-boiled & blackened
yolk of his body split, right there
on stage, you couldn't help
yourself. What instrument,
the eye sans the heart.
Yes, discernible; say sagacious
even in this dark. But who
first fancied the question
in silk, who bid him to dress
in skin-tight, pinstriped pantaloons,
topped it with a pillbox hat,
precarious as a popped soda cap,
who gave him a handle
like Oleander or Linoleum?

But Butter starts anyway, twisting
like the lining of his liver done
just caught fire; Butter, crooning some
murky cool. All that hurt & history
steady pulling like a gandy-dancer
long held prisoner behind the curtain,
& forever working, working its way
to the surface of the skin.

Senegambian Carnival

Enter the sidesplitter,
     & the new further adventures

of Dollar Bill. The plum, plumed
     sunset, a spiraling starburst of black

& tan, a begloomed bouquet of legs,
     like sectioned breadfruit, the color

of crushed star anise. Straight from speck
     to spectacle, from buckskin to mink

& black sable, this hackneyed honey.
     Gaslit, murksome. Epidermic & episodic,

the curtain, a velvet maidenhead, a velum
     of smoke, the midmost membrane between

this body & brain.

He's His Own Grandfather

And if you ask the genealogist—
it's all pie chart and phylum, some
enigmatic sequence of amino acid
and event, an anagram, or some kind
of backwoods and backward cartography
of the blood. A colored conundrum
of cousins, and sister-cousins, relations
to dead relations, and the extra-ordinary
philanderings of an ex-short-term
family friend. Of fruit, my stock is teeming.
And I'll be the first to admit, the bark,
the boughs are full and still blooming
on my proverbial little tree.

Cork

Falconer Blanc de Noir Krug Grand Cuvee Falconer Blanc de Blanc Russian River Domaine Chandon Brut Moet & Chandon Nectar Imperial Moet & Chandon White Star Pommery Brut Rose Jubilee Clorindy Domaine Chandon Pick Blanc de Noirs Roederer Estate L'Hermitage Brut Pompey Veuve Clicquot Demi-Sec Sissle King San Giovanni Prosecco Crow Heidsieck Monopole Yellow Brut Andre Egbert Brut Domaine J. Lassalle Brut Imperial & Wing Rag Freixenet Cordon Negro Brut Freixenet Cordon Negro Extra Dry Buck Graham Beck Blanc de Blancs Shuffle Andre Cold Duck Dahomey Heidsieck Monopole Diamant Bleu Ethiop Shipp Jacquesson & Fils Brut Crow Signature Jim Juve Y Camps Gran Guve Y Camps Brut Quick Laurent Perrier Brut Step Louis Roederer Cristal Mionetto Il Prosecco Rose Bandana Moet & Chandon Sissieretta Dom Perignon Moncuit Blanc de Blanc Grand Cru Crow Coleville Veuve Clicquot La Grand Dame Zip Wolffer Brut Virginny Villa Rosa Jonah Barolo Poor Pour Po Zardetto di Prosecco Grappa Ziegfield Zardetto Prosecco di Conegliano Brut Heel Toe Heel Toe Heel Toe Heel Toe Hell Toe To Heel Toe Heel Toe Heel Toe Toe Heel Hell He'll Heal Tow Heal Tow Toe He'll Heal Too.

Unholy

". . . to break, blow, burn, and make me new."

—John Donne

Batter my aunt, three-pancake girl; a store
Of fat bubbling across the floor. Near
Fifty—red, white, pale—long gone, my father's
Sister, my mirror. He missed her. Please hear
Me. Answer me. Black is not the question.
Jemima's wears? See Jemima's red roll,
Her monkey. Depart! Miss this reflection!
"A display pays, girl." A bandanna, please.
A buck? Sisters live and the family haunts.
Nineteen nieces. Don an apron. Cook. This
Is not, cannot be the ladder. Hold on.
Own this eye. See. Or lease a white mirror.
Rent-a-Jemima (the black bubbling).
Rent-a-Jemima, and hold fast to bling.

Joe Louis Was a Motherfucker

You had to see this nigga in action, jack. Starlight in his hands. Diamond studded starlight, the kind you might find stuck between Elizabeth Taylor's toes. The sound of salted leather & flesh was staccato. And pretty, this nigga was like triple-dipped, gold-plated honey, bright as a new penny pulled from the pocket of Dwight D. the day he thought he'd lost to Dewey. Pretty. You'd watch him pigeon hawk some turkey like a titmouse, then he'd be all up on 125th armed with a turtledove, spatted, gabardine suited & booted, his handkerchief, sky-peach to match his tiepin and cuffs. I hope he had onion breath; that that nigga's hemorrhoids made his ass feel like a burlap sack full of rock salt. That Joe Louis, he sure was a motherfucker & beautiful.

The Further Adventures of Long Dong Silver (or The Incredible Tale of a Boy's Perilous Journey from Pin Point to the Chocolate City) as Told to Anita Hill

After the shower scene, San Pedro, circa 1983

Meanwhile, we find our hero
romancing a little Arm & Hammer
along the business end of his toothbrush.

But, it's the thrum and weight of all
that music, like some fist, anonymous
and dying against the bass drum of your throat.

As viewer, you are asked to consider all those
angles, the soft edges, the high cut and gloss
of his Thriller jacket. Aside from his hair,

you are prepared to call the whole damn thing
a hoax, evidence of some early prosthesis,
maybe even a little expert sleight of hand.

This must be a monster of mirrors.
There's the scientist looming beyond the steam.

Colored American Day

The White City, 1893

They shuffle along, gliding through the pine straw
And peanut shells, the dust settling almost like
Cloud-cover around their feet. The children's painted
Faces, their sticky mouths, their hands melting—
Yes, we danced for them. In passing, a boy says,
"You have the whitest teeth I've every seen."
In this sea of curiosities, our skin like smoked
Glass on display. The main attraction,
Edison's box of light and the miracle of those
Electric men. The contortionist, the Sioux's Ghost
Dance, the woman bathing her baby in a tub of milk.
The sun, pitched like a high-hat at the horizon,
The shadows are calico, the night like a hitched hem.

An Epistemology of Ralph Ellison's Articulation of the Blues as Explained by Mantan Moreland

My shoes is an episode, near aspic, near chronic,
Musketeering, the tragic train. These clues, an impulse
To sleep, to keep alive when one's baking sausages.
To keep the poodle experiments alive, to finger their scruffy
Mane and transgender it, not by cancellation of photography
At home, but through squeezing from it, a near orgasmic,
Near cosmic cynicism.

Ars Poetica as Phrenology
(or Phrenology as Ars Poetica)

So here's the bit, my shtick,
To make my mouth a miliary,

To wade through this muddy
Morphology, to get all buck

And wing, volley those notes
Into the spotlight and sing. O,

My hippocampus is hawkish.

And if you wanna go exoskeletal,
Or get all "the cranium's vault,"

Or how the crest is swaybacked
And prismatic—well, when push

Comes to shove, I can get
Downright Aeolian on you, son.

On Behalf of the Brotherhood of Odd Fellows, The Sepia Players Present: The Blackbirds

but first . . .

"if Gandhi were a New Yorker
he would never fast. ZUCCA's
tempting dishes would lure
him to the Gardens daily. You
too will find ZUCCA's dishes
delicious"

and remember there are chocolates
for sale in the lobby

Cue Master Nicholas, Harold at fourteen,
a jig-saw of legs, oblong elbows akimbo—
a bedlam, quick as an oil slick of Kongolene.

The *Inter-State Tattler* will tell you:
Ring shout, wheel about, strut, then stare,
how could a boy so young adulterate the air.

My coloratura dreamland, and all this business
of jubilee. Midnight rooftop bacchanals
and the Dance of Salome. O, the showgirls

and ponies, something for everyone to see,
the Darktown Follies of San Juan Hill or
"At the Howard" in D.C. Who can do The Buzzard

Loop, The Snakehips was serpentine, Stand
& Shimmy, or Ballin' the Jack, even The Fish Tale
was mean. Butterbeans and Susie, Fisk's

"Ezekiel Saw the Wheel," the deaths
of Florence Mills and Mary Cahill.
"Cupid was an Indian Pickaninny,"

"The Wedding of the Chinee and the Coon,"
"Who Dat Say Chicken in Dis Crowd,"
and "The Maid of Timbuctoo."

At the Gaiety in London, they're gathering
right now. Grandmas, tots, and poodles
will pepper the crowd. TOBY: tough

on black actors, tough on black asses,
and tired of being abused, while the porters
and the bootblacks are whistling Handy's Blues.

Read *The Defender, The Indianapolis Freemen*
you'll see what I mean, Edison's removable wax
cylinders and that Victor Talking Machine.

THE OLIO

"As one strawberry said to the other:
if we hadn't been in that bed together,
we wouldn't be in this jam now."

—Jackie "Moms" Mabley

Approaching Thunder

Let's assume about the body
that after applying enough pressure
it could, same as the cottonwood,
or the limbs of that damn box elder,
the one our neighbors kept calling

a weed; how that night, the worst
of the summer storms spread its fingers
across the little piece of earth and air
we thought we owned, how it took
each tree by the throat and turned.

Yes, I remember the first night
I guilted you into making love,
how the color of the stone changed
in your eye each time I touched;
how silence rose from your skin,

began to accumulate above our heads.
And for hours we lay still, listening
to the wind opening and closing
its purple fists. Then come morning,
we took an inventory of what we'd lost.

Tired Blood

Early stage, the old folks would have noticed
the sheen of metal flaking beneath her skin,
and thought how on the darkest nights of winter,
when cat and smallmouth bass felt safe enough
to take a quick breath, the air seemed to steady
its palm on the crown of the moon, and hold it
just so below the surface of the Brazos River.

When the X-rays came back, we saw Mother
looking like she'd been eased up in the corner
of some red-lit room, Jim Beam and dip tobacco
flavoring each shadow, loud-talk and cussing,
cards like the glint of straight-razors, that image,
like she'd been shifting weight with the Devil
long enough for him to whisper his real name
in her mouth, leave his handprint along her waist.

Orange Country Fair

Aside from the bustling farm life
and the funnel cake and the screams
spinning down from the Jackhammer
and, of course, the ceremonial milking
of the oreo cow, aside from the surprising
absence of pink on the prize-winning pig's
nose, O, and that amazing and vibrating
chick-thick egg and the way the chicks
as a whole started to look a little like
corn muffins, but we were getting hungry
by then, and had already weighed
the benefits between tropical and chocolate
topping, and the stilt-walker dressed
as Abe Lincoln and the stilt-walker
dressed as Jackie Robinson were taking
a smoke, and maybe the sword-swallower
was taking a shit; once my father stuck
a curtain rod down his throat, but we were
never that dumb, we were kids, we were
hot and bored, and all the lines were long.

Featured at the Borghese, Contrition

Having not considered Caravaggio,
even with the Levis so neatly tucked
in my back pocket, and having already
acquired my own special brand
of sweetness and melancholy and horror,
I stood in line. And to my discredit,
all week all the sidewalks pointed
one direction. The tote bags and foam
figurines: self-portrait as rocket, man as
Medusa's hurled and descending head.

I'd worried about not having
enough coin in my pocket to pee.
And after The God Show at the Vatican,
and hedging my bets along the length
of black Peter's prayer-polished toes,
I found myself lost. Sure enough,
Borghese ripped my ticket,
and from the onset, there was blood
and beauty, and of course, your above-
average bouquet of boy whores.

This was Rome. This is Rome,
still. And this curious attention
to cut figs, an oblong dark, their
under-ripe and pit-less hearts.
And all around the city this celebrated
dark. And this poem after a poem
after a poem on where I stood.
And where the light fell on David's
outstretched arm, and everyone
reading into the Giant's eyes.

Le Cinque Terre

In Vernazza, it's hillside—a wind
unfolding its hand against a creamy
brushwork of black and white. I was
alone, and I had been alone: dancing,
sidestepping the cliff's edge
from Monterosso al Mare, stumbling
and almost courting the footnote
of another poet's death. You fool. Skin
as scaffolding, the delicate angularity
of your neck and hands. The simple
music we rush to scratch from our heads.
Where will you walk tonight, Craig Arnold?
Here, the trail way is terraced with grapevines,
it descends into a palm-shaped, pocketed
harbor, where children leap from a jetty
into the harbor's pan-sifted light,
where the Brits become unbearably red.

Midnight at the Abandoned Monastery

We were reluctant to walk.
The last few glasses of vino
Had tinted the dying Tuscan sky.
But enough were game, so
The girls changed into their sensible
Shoes, and the overly prepared,
Who bragged about bow hunting
And the shades of deer blood
Near their Virginia home, had packed
Plenty of headlamps to please the mob.

The full moon with its pockets
Of light, sometimes carving its own
Path, its machinery, stretching out
Like another Roman road into the minor
Histories of night. I'd like to think
We stunned the black locusts
Into silence and the electric fence
Was enough to lull the hogs
And cattle into their sleep.

We were warned of the packs
Of wild boar, and how a farmer had
Happened upon her dear devoured dog.
The dips and hills, the bad jokes,
The sections of gravel, loose stones
And uneasy laughter were not
All that made our journey long.

Soon there was only the gulf
Of our footsteps, our breathing taunt

And brittle as string. Approaching the wall
Seemed like swimming against the hull
Of some long-scuttled ship. We entered
Half expecting the wild mint that
Choked the courtyard to be rockweed
Or plankton. We hung from the arched
Windows and tap-danced around
Stairwells, the partially collapsed floors,
Cloaked in our weak knowledge of the fashions
Of architectural history. Before spitting,
The cistern seemed like a clear black death.
All the graffitied hearts and cocks, the one god,
The hundreds of generations of men.

8 ½

Maybe it wasn't the whip
　　　that made the whole scene

seem almost un-filmable, or how
　　　so quickly, the feathers took on
the chemical properties of foam.

O, as expected, the women
　　　were bubbly, even while working

to spoon out the egg-like lover
　　　from a wooden tub. Of course,

they dress and powder him. They
　　　sling him between them, marching

jazz-like as pallbearers
　　　to an inaudible tune.

From her stained teeth and bowed
　　　legs, her broken dance, we know
the French showgirl is done.

So enters the Black with a scissor
　　　kick, a jackknifed foot, semblance

of her imagined native waltz. His wide
　　　brimmed hat, his catwalk. The dark

half-curl ironed flat against her brow,
　　　beckoning like a hook.

Lament

When I die, I want the white rush
of your name to flood my ear.

I want the color of wheat stripped
clean from the air, except, of course—

the exceptional smell of sun lingering
on the fabric of your skin.

When I'm gone, my dear: wash my body
on the coastline, where the stones

still litter the sand like relics
of some nameless nation of the blind.

Wash me, where we wallowed in salt,
where we slapped and wailed like seals.

I want to pull the hour
from the mouth of the day

And I'll return as rain
and the gathering dust about the house.

I know I'm good. I'll find a way
to be good to you again.

Mister Dramatic

1.

You carry that note,

            crystalline

almost diaphanous—

as if the sound itself
                was stemware,

         or ornamental—

recessed,
          & set high enough

on a shelf to ward off
          even

the possibility of travel.

It's almost as if
          in some unspoken

or unspeakable

way,   you sidestepped

that otherwise uneventful moment

which ends every boyhood,

         when a certain pitch,

slightly ethereal,

       almost ecclesiastic,

assumes the simple properties

of air.

2.

Part beacon,   part balefire now,

which lulls,

       coaxes the heart

to stagger,   to careen,

founder against the crags,

       to court calamity along

some lamp lit & frozen

       inner city curb.

Your voice adrift   the voice box

    a box kite clinging to

that golden key.

Wine with Hula Hoop

I'm a good husband and father
and I think an honest man,
so why do I feel so lascivious?
I know that I know so much
more than these twenty something
girls: the hips' recreational apparatus,
the glass, this buttery accumulation
of light. When they speak I can't speak.
I hold the whole word in my mouth
like an apple, a worm, and its core.

Afternoon at the First King

And the men again are marbling
Their money, which falls where
The light falls, near the pole
And that ever extending elongated
V of the groin. The manufactured night.
The gold dust and jasmine body
Spray, hanging and sparkling like
Silica in the lungs. No one ever
Notices the stillness of men,
Paralyzed, at least partially, by
A patina of the skin. A geometry,
Convex, oblong. Then the sudden
And biting smell of wings.

Before I Let Go

Already they were singing
into the upturned tubes of lipstick
at the vanities of their rented
rooms, singing, lined outside
a second-degree VIP parking,
or frozen in the new geometry
of a Polaroid pose, where someone's
used bed sheet becomes an airbrushed,
Cadillac-bracketed midnight.

What do you know about purple
on purple suits & drinking French
Connections, the arena's artificial smoke,
a mix between tobacco sweet & a matted
gun-barrel black. Then Frankie sings:
& it's like the edge or inverse of a tremor
you may have felt once in the back pew
of a Double Rock, Mt. Vernon, Greater
Brenian Holiness Baptist Baptist Church.

Frankie, only & always dressed in white,
pressed like new money, clean as the original
pope of R&B. Those thousands of willing,
ready & able women, set for one man,
might settle for making love to me.

In the Absence of Laughter

maybe, because the room took

the smell of wet clay

or carnations

graying somewhere, like

for instance, beside the nightstand

or tucked in a few loose bundles

beneath his twin bed

and with all the blinds drawn

anyway, and the air

the color of iron ore, maybe

it was easy, especially

with the accumulation of salt

against the tongue, spiral of blood

swelling the inner ear and nostrils

and the other boys, waiting—

it was easy, in the absence

of laughter,

to miss exactly what

she said.

The Bell Curve

It must be such a burden,
all that grace and muscle.

The white horse breaking
loose from its stall. The ridge

line arching away like the man
thumbing his blade beneath

the skin of an apple.
Thinking, too, of beauty . . .

your back angling away
like a line of sight. The children

slinging their paper arrows
at the sun, piercing the light

until it bleeds gold. Until it bleeds.

Dusk in Andalusia

The fireflies are set to riot.
Every town washed the color of ash
And soon they will lean their torches
Against the long grass of the hillside,
And stretch for the boughs of orange trees,
Then up into the eucalyptus and the ivy
Along the walls of the Alhambra until
There is nothing left recognizable of night.

Their blank faces tell the history of Granada,
Where the weight of scented oil, worn leather
And rosemary burning hangs in the air.
Song like a quarter of fruit lodged
In a woman's throat, and then an explosion
Or the sound of uncontrollable laughter.

Fifteenth Street is Burning

The beating I took from my father
came the same year a storm tore
down half the palm trees at the park;

rained so, until the water reached
the third step, and all the perennials
mother planted, bunched basket-of-gold,

the asters, the blood-red geranium,
their roots caught and discolored
like fingers clutching the fence.

I don't remember the first thing I burned,
but I still see how the color claimed it;
pear-shaped for a moment, almost small

enough to hold, until the flame opened
its mouth, cut loose a sound, and slipped
free from its slender yoke. Gone, the time

for remembering when mama said never
let a stranger in the house. So when daddy
came through the door, and the fire was out,

it was all he could think to do.

Center Your Scalpel

here   along the breastbone—

never mind   about the blood

not skin   my cup and bowl   not

the darker tributaries   of the body

that   lesser sweetness   hard

fought for   and rarely   won

held prisoner   like two songbirds

damn near   the size of a grown man's

fists.   Their coupling

like the sound   of a claw-hammer

against an iron door.

The Faithful Groomsman

Mid-December it starts: the swells, high
As welts along the surface of the river,
The wash spitting over the rocks,
Threatening to crest the Jersey shore.

We don't know where the Party crossed.
In Düsseldorf, the artist lost possibly
To nostalgia, imagined the Durham boats,
An assembly of oarsmen thwacking
Ice floes. Washington's regalia, his profile.

Consider the rumor of the boy left holding
The reigns of his prize Palomino, Blueskin.
The first reports were about the boy's pallor,
Then all those misinterpretations of the boy's face,
A subtle contortion someone decided to call a smile.

Marceline's Sermon

Guyana, 1978

You see, his gift was healing.
And to look upon him, to spy
Him in the pulpit, at the figure
Of a man he cut, and notice how
His face lit the shadows beneath
The tent; how, even in that heat
The shirts I laid for him seemed
To never lose their crease,
And then he spoke, and all at once
We knew of the presence of God.

I knew of the children he fathered,
And all the other women, devotees
Who, of their own free will, decided
To unburden themselves of sin,
Selling most of their worldly goods,
And giving what they could not carry.
When asked, he said to comfort them
Was part the business of the body,
To ease the suffering of the flesh,
What soon we all will leave behind.

Redondo at Dusk

Heat in the blood. My blindfold. The bone-shutters wrenched shut.
This wax-white layer like a caul. Heat in the blood. This pounding,
this fire tunneling, a tornado tipped on its edge. The sun like a sinkhole
in the flesh, or where the river, the musky, ink-black and broken shore

swings its hammer. The Farmers' Almanac foretold disaster, how the clouds
might ignite, turn mulberry and gush. So we stoned the sunlight from our eyes.
We boiled our hands. We drank deep from our chests. We sang. We sang. We.

Last Night in Mattapan

It's easier still to think *mercy,*
blood in the urine, the bowed legs,
the all night, childlike *yelp, yelp,*
the dog's liver, bright and tender
as a balloon. So when the farmer
leads him out with a bowl of crushed
apples, through the field stubble
and mulch, we can't help ourselves.
And how tender, and almost loving,
becomes the lone report, scattering
the crows into shards of black glass.

In the movie, the parents smoke
hash—the father, half-reading
Reagan, the President and the Man.
And this we assume becomes
a prelude: lamplight dissolving
into moonlight, then, of course,
into a shadowed, airbrushed
imagining of their making love.
So when the phantom takes
the little girl, chooses the child
first, we are meant to feel
their anguish and guilt, learn
to study the colorless face,
Craig T. Nelson's receding hairline,
his furrowed brow.

I want to believe there is still
hesitation in the world. Yes,
cruelty or mercy, as it must,
will run its course. And maybe

it's easier to say the Racine man
who hacked down his family
over coffee was just insane. The note
beneath the newscaster's voice:
what a pity, what a waste of skin.

And in Mattapan, let's give
them, too, the benefit of doubt,
that maybe what the killers
wanted more than anything
was the gift of silence. Choose.
You have to choose, to witness.
One drags the half-dressed
woman by her hair down
the stoop. Another says, *I'll carry*
the baby, and take care of the baby too.
We know what the media fancies,
this wet work, like a propensity
for sweets. And all I kept asking:
how old when a child understands
that the stakes are too high for tears,
when does she gather herself, beg.

Ruby Bates: I Think I Love You

Scottsboro

I can be your boxcar dark, and our eyes—
standing, lit and still as settled coal.
I'll be your wind-drawn psalm, a quiver
from the gap at the door. I can be a beaded
night, that catgut, the fruit-laden bough
in another broke-down Alabama song.
So don't you doddle now, darling. We'll
marshal this bale, our bunk. Can't you
feel how the hound dogs tussle and pull
in the ragweed, chasing the arclight, the low
swinging lamplight. Don't you worry none
about that matted hair. The rail's iron lip,
its hum, the double-click like a tongue,
or the hammer of a just-cocked gun.

Cherene

We've finished the bread; we'll end the meal with a taste of pomegranate.
I'll twist the moon from its vine & measure its weight against a pomegranate's.

After sampling the smoke in your skin, my lips were cured. Smiling,
I gulped the air, my throat red, ballooning to the size of a pomegranate.

When the house is empty, I stand at the window. Our cat yelps
like a dog at the door, & this silence reeks of rotting pomegranate.

Last night was as dark as dried blood. When you carried our son
you dreamed of an orchard where skulls were as small as pomegranates.

I keep company with shadows. We sit in the living room,
I offer wine & cheese, & apologize for the absence of pomegranate.

Late, when my mother was gone, I counted the passing cars
from the front porch; taillights like seeds spit from a pomegranate.

A modern romance. You undress, but never say a word.
I touch your ribcage, take my thumbs, & split you like a pomegranate.

Notes

"Two Real Coons" refers to the title of an 1896 musical, starring Bert Williams and George Walker.

"LeRoi Eating Watermelon at Howard" references Amiri Baraka, formerly known as LeRoi Jones.

"Miss Thelma" refers to Thelma "Butterfly" McQueen, who is best known for her role as Prissy in *Gone with the Wind.*

"Fancywork" references Sissieretta Jones, also known as "The Black Patti" after Adelina Patti, an Italian soprano.

"Pigmeat" references the comedian, Dewey "Pigmeat" Markham, who recorded the hit song "Here Comes the Judge" in 1968.

Lucy Jane Stubbles was the love interest of Ernest Hogan, a songwriter and comedian during the Vaudeville era. Ms. Stubbles was the inspiration for his infamous hit song, "All Coons Look Alike to Me," which was originally titled "All Pimps Look Alike to Me."

In "Then Butterbeans Begins 'The Itch,'" Butterbeans refers to one member of the comedic husband and wife duo, Butterbeans and Susie.

"Unholy" is after "Ladders" by Elizabeth Alexander.

"Joe Louis Was a Motherfucker" is for Angela Jackson and Tyehimba Jess.

"An Epistemology of Ralph Ellison's Articulation of the Blues as Explained by Mantan Moreland" is after Harryette Mullen and Terrance Hayes.

"Tired Blood" is for Nellie McKay.

"Featured at The Borghese, Contrition" is after Paul Otremba.

"Le Cinque Terre" references Craig Arnold, a poet who disappeared during a solo hike in Japan in 2009.

"8½" refers to Federico Fellini's 1963 film of the same title.

"Lament" is after Neruda.

"The Faithful Groomsman" references the story of Jocko Graves, a twelve-year-old boy, who in 1776 froze to death while holding George Washington's horse Blueskin as the general famously crossed the Delaware River.

"Marceline's Sermon" refers to Marceline Jones, wife of Jim Jones, leader of The People's Temple and the Jonestown Massacre.

"Ruby Bates" refers to one of the two accusers of the Scottsboro Boys of 1931.

Acknowledgments

Versions of these poems have appeared in the following journals:

Anti-: "An Epistemology of Ralph Ellison's Articulation of the Blues as Explained by Mantan Moreland," "It's the Kingfish, Honey—Pining," and "Joe Louis Was a Motherfucker."

Copper Nickel: "8½," "Mister Dramatic," and "Ruby Bates: I Think I Love You."

Eleven Eleven: "Clarence Muse Stars as The Magical Negro in Francis Ford Coppola's *The Black Stallion* (1979)" and "Senegambian Carnival."

Harvard Review: "On Behalf of the Brotherhood of Odd Fellows, The Sepia Players Present: The Blackbirds."

Indiana Review: "Bootlick," "Miss Thelma," "Nobody," "Pigmeat," and "Two Real Coons."

Kweli Journal: "Last Night in Mattapan."

Muckworks: "Unholy."

Narrative Magazine: "Ars Poetica as Phrenology (or Phrenology as Ars Poetica)," "A Blues for Miss Lucy Jane Stubbles," "Featured at The Borghese, Contrition," "He's His Own Grandfather," "Le Cinque Terre," and "Midnight at the Abandoned Monastery."

Quarterly West: "He Swallowed an Egg."

Shenandoah: "LeRoi Eating Watermelon at Howard" and "Tired Blood."

The Southern Review: "Approaching Thunder," "Cherene," and "Then Butterbeans Begins 'The Itch.'"

Verse Daily: "Approaching Thunder."

Waccamaw: "The Front Matter" and "Orange County Fair."

West Branch: "Encore" and "Fancywork."

I am eternally grateful for the support of my family, friends, and colleagues. Your guidance, grace, and understanding made this work possible. I would like to thank Terrance Hayes, Carl Phillips, Douglas Kearney, Shara Lessley, Matthew Shenoda, Stephen and Jade Webber, Jim Schley, Jeffrey Levine, The Program in Creative Writing at the University of Wisconsin–Madison, The Bread Loaf Writers' Conference, The Spannocchia Foundation, and the National Endowment for the Arts. Words fail to express my gratitude for the love and support of my wife, Cherene Sherrard. The bulk of this book was written in stolen hours or during sixty-minute coffee shop fellowships underwritten by sacrifices she made. Thank you, again.

Other books from Tupelo Press

Fasting for Ramadan: Notes from a Spiritual Practice (memoir), Kazim Ali
This Lamentable City (poems), Polina Barskova, edited by Ilya Kaminsky
Circle's Apprentice (poems), Dan Beachy-Quick
The Vital System (poems), CM Burroughs
Stone Lyre: Poems of René Char, translated by Nancy Naomi Carlson
Severance Songs (poems), Joshua Corey
Atlas Hour (poems), Carol Ann Davis
New Cathay: Contemporary Chinese Poetry, edited by Ming Di
Sanderlings (poems), Geri Doran
The Flight Cage (poems), Rebecca Dunham
The Posthumous Affair (novel), James Friel
Nothing Can Make Me Do This (novel), David Huddle
Meridian (poems), Kathleen Jesme
Darktown Follies (poems), Amaud Jamaul Johnson
Dancing in Odessa (poems), Ilya Kaminsky
A God in the House: Poets Talk About Faith (interviews),
    edited by Ilya Kaminsky and Katherine Towler
Manoleria (poems), Daniel Khalastchi
domina Un/blued (poems), Ruth Ellen Kocher
Phyla of Joy (poems), Karen An-hwei Lee
Engraved (poems), Anna George Meek
Body Thesaurus (poems), Jennifer Militello
Mary & the Giant Mechanism (poems), Mary Molinary
After Urgency (poems), Rusty Morrison
Lucky Fish (poems), Aimee Nezhukumatathil
Long Division (poems), Alan Michael Parker
Ex-Voto (poems), Adélia Prado, translated by Ellen Doré Watson
Intimate: An American Family Photo Album (memoir), Paisley Rekdal
Thrill-Bent (novel), Jan Richman
Calendars of Fire (poems), Lee Sharkey
Cream of Kohlrabi: Stories, Floyd Skloot
The Perfect Life (essays), Peter Stitt
Swallowing the Sea (essays), Lee Upton
Butch Geography (poems), Stacey Waite
Dogged Hearts (poems), Ellen Doré Watson

See our complete backlist at www.tupelopress.org